Coming Home

Samantha Wood-Gaines

BookLeaf
Publishing

India | USA | UK

Presentation by *BookLeaf Publishing*

Web: www.bookleafpub.com

E-mail: info@bookleafpub.com

ISBN : 9789358362008

First edition 2021

May this be a place you can feel something.

Acknowledgement

Thank you to my parents for always supporting me and allowing me to express myself creatively. I am beyond thankful to be able to live out my life going after my dreams with the full support of my family, friends and my beautiful partner. With this support, I feel like I can achieve anything I put my mind to. I have so much love for you all.

Let The Pieces Fall

Let the pieces fall where they may,

As the trees whistle and sway,

I'm in my head thinking of all the ways,

The way things used to be,

When things were high strung,

Now feeling like I've got water in my lungs,

It's hard to breathe

But that's just anxiety,

Whispering in my ear,

Trying to tap into fear,

When these thoughts start to crowd,

I stop and listen to the sound,

The sounds of the ocean,

It is the ocean that calls my name.

Lost and Found

Sweet like a songbird,

Travelling through the woods,

There is a lost girl,

Trying to get home,

I reach out my hand and realize,

She's a distant memory of me,

I see my past self,

My younger self,

Scared, but still choosing

To be brave,

Brave enough to weather the storm,

Strong enough to dredge through the waters,

To get to the other side,

To get to the light,

She continues to make strides,

Holding onto hope,

For a better tomorrow.

Ocean Dance

Sunshine shimmers like diamonds,

They reflect off the ocean,

And jump along the waves,

The wind tirelessly teases

My curly locks,

These locks dance in the sky,

Dancing above my head,

Reaching to touch the sun,

The sun brings me out to the ocean,

And staring at the ocean stops time,

This is where I find my peace,

This is where I meet my most honest self,

For the ocean is my home.

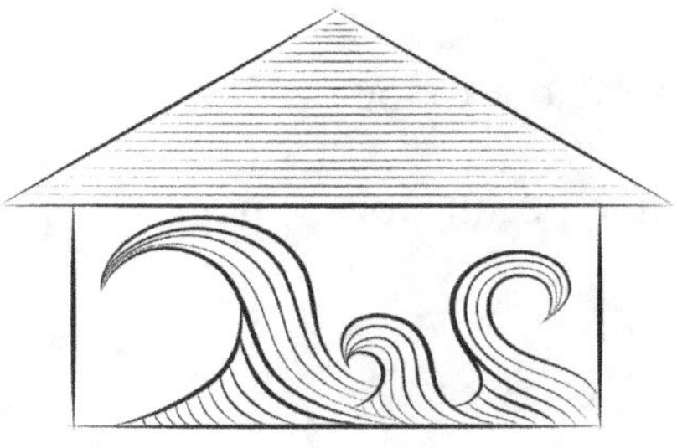

Cloudy With a Chance of Rain

Thick grey clouds rush in

To hide yesterday's heat,

With a cool breeze,

A breeze I'd almost forgotten,

It taps me on my shoulder,

Sending shivers down my spine,

Rain comes to me,

Feeding the trees

Trees that feed us oxygen

To fill our lungs,

The cool wind brushes my face.

While rain feels cold and tiring,

It also feels cozy and comforting.

So you see,

Rain must come,

There must be a balance,

With balance comes abundance,

Just one of Mother Nature's little gifts.

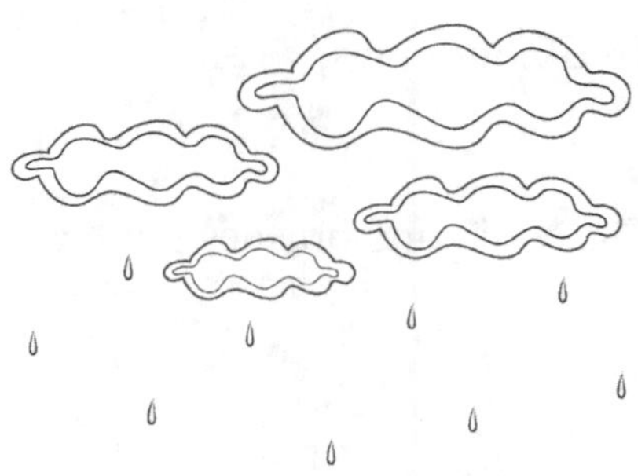

Beware of Fleeting Memories

Pieces from our past

May linger longer than anticipated.

Sometimes we don't realize

How many memories tag along,

The times we believe

We've overcome our past

Can also be the very moment

We find ourselves drowning in memories.

Unable to understand

The why's of yesterday,

We are reminded that healing

Is not a one time occurrence.

Healing is an option,

A decision we must choose

Again and again, and work hard at

Maintaining our peace every day.

As our brains tend to play tricks on us

And fool us easily,

In sparking old flames or forgotten rage,

Remember that not all thoughts are true:

No emotion is 'right' or 'wrong.'

Feel things as they come,

And keep flowing like the ocean.

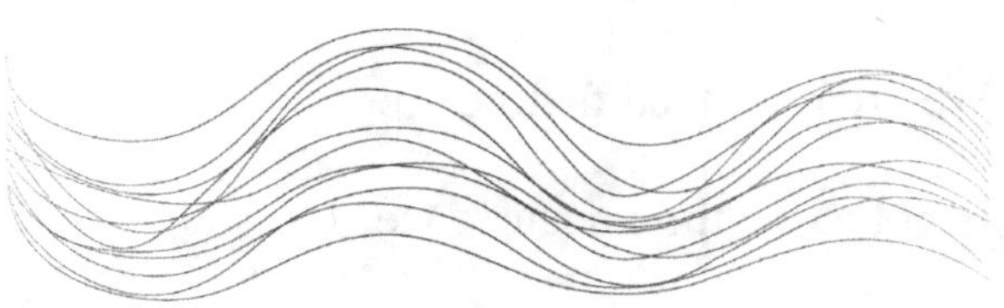

The Vast Unknown

Sky full of stars

Laid out like a map,

A never ending maze

To a place we never met,

Following that True North,

Leading us to somewhere new,

I know that we remain here

For a greater purpose,

Who are we to question

The great universe and

Every secret she holds,

Much like our dreams,

There is a vast unknown,

With more stars in the sky

Than grains of sand on Earth,

I reminisce about

The small things in life.

Sunsets By The Sea

The tide is swiftly drifting in,

To soak my feet and pull me in closer again,

It attempts to convince me

To stay in its cool blue oasis,

I allow its urgent pull.

I disrobe and sink into the ocean,

As I am called to swim to the dock,

I watch the sunset sparkle upon

Meeting the deep blue sea,

Golden on every inch of my skin,

I soak up the last light of the day,

In absorbing this moment,

I am one with the sea.

Tale Of The Water Dog

I pull the leash,

Trying to convince our dog

To part ways with the ocean.

He stares up at me

With loving eyes and stands with

The stubbornness of a horse.

He now signals that he wants to stay,

As he always does when it's time to leave,

Peering out into the field

Of neverending waves,

He whimpers and begs to stay

Only for a moment longer.

With such a sweet face,

Like a field of sunflowers,

He never fails to brighten my day.

So I give in one last time,

And power my last throw,

To satisfy his undying love

For that cool blue ocean rush.

Cotton Candy Skies

While the world can be unsettling at times,

I feel grounded by cotton candy skies,

The swatches of pink and purple

Weave through the pale blue sky,

The ocean's crashing waves

Tumble and fall at my feet,

The flowers smell fresh like spring,

Their lively color, painting the streets.

Oh, how I love cotton candy skies.

Through All Of My Seasons

Loving me through all of my seasons,

Allows me to be my truest self,

It is freeing and encouraging,

Allowing me to spread my wings
And achieve my wildest dreams.

This kind of love comes to me every day,

It does not take anything away from me,

It only fills every ounce of my soul.

Sometimes this love looks like:

Cooking dinner together

While dancing in the kitchen,

Kisses in bed before leaving for work,

Allowing our bodies to flow and stretch

While listening to soothing music,

Allowing each other to be heard,

and allowing space for time apart,

These habits make up a big part

Of our everyday expression of love,

The simple act of loving each other,

Through all of our seasons.

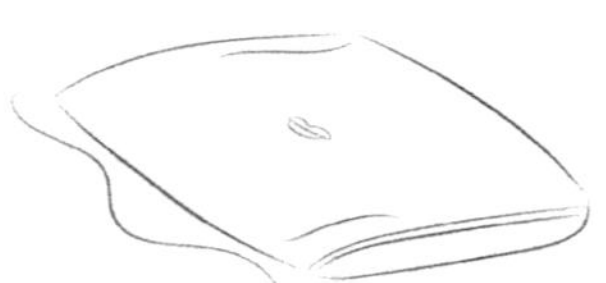

Great Escape

Tranquility rushes through me

As I soften my gaze,

The breath of the earth

Creates my escape,

An escape from the city,

A breakaway from normalcy,

I allow myself to be consumed

By nature's warm embrace.

Dear Stubborn Curls

Oh how I love you,

My dearest messy curls,

After all I have invested,

You still have a mind of your own,

And still have great strength in

Resisting a comb.

And I remember how

I used to get so angry at you,

As you'd always pick a fight,

Although I hated you at times,

I learned how to take care of you.

I gave you some grace,

Kept my cool while tirelessly

Working hard to style you,

But you did your own thing,

And I learned to accept you,

For all that you are,

What a journey it's been.

Less Is Not More Here

You're scared of

Being vulnerable,

I get it,

You confirm

Your worst fears,

And feel as through

You can't find happiness

Within yourself.

So you sabotage

What you do have

In order to feel better

About being alone.

But denying good

Things in your life

By hurting others

Only causes more damage,

You alienate yourself,

You force yourself

To care less,

To feel less,

To do less,

But less is not more here.

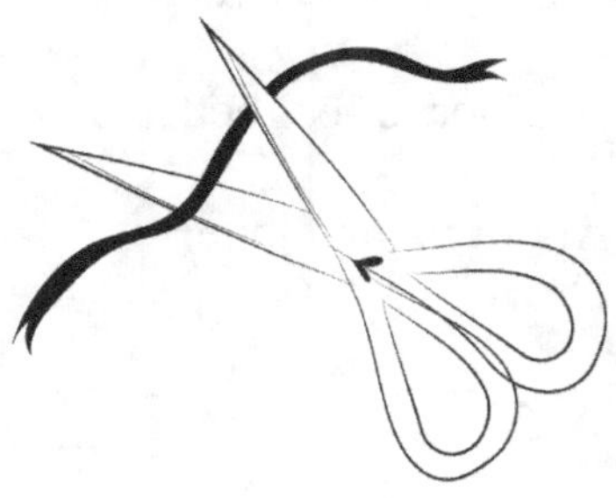

Gloomy Days

A stillness occurs for a moment,

As a cold breeze crawls into the room,

I look out my window and

See the dark grey clouds,

Raindrops fall to soak the ground,

Green is the only color I see,

Gloomy days like these

Remind me that the sun

Doesn't need to shine

For me to be happy,

I am happy in my little room,

With my dog sleeping next to me,

Sipping my tea in hand.

I don't need the sunshine

To bring me laughter,

Laughter comes to me when

My partner makes funny accents,

Playing footsie under the table

While enjoying a late night dinner,

These gloomy days are necessary,

They allow me to slow down and focus

On what is right in front of me.

My Forever Home

When I'm in your arms,

The stars seem so much brighter,

As you pull me in, closer to your chest,

I feel your breath tickle my neck,

I'm able to hear your heart beating,

Steadily and strong against my ear,

As I turn to look up at you,

Your smile shines brighter than the sun,

I kiss you tenderly as I crave

Your lips touching mine,

You kiss my forehead

And hug me dearly,

You are my forever home.

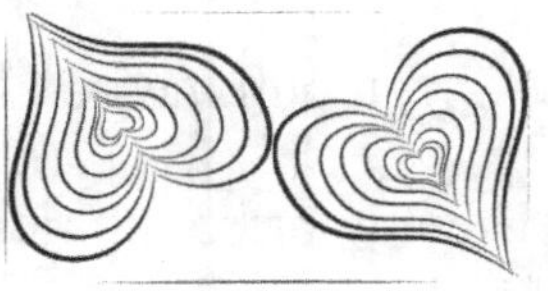

In My Loneliest Hours

I used to feel so alone,

As if the world had

Forgotten about me,

Sometimes I knew this wasn't true

While other times, that idea felt too real,

It became hard to know myself and

What I really wanted out of this life,

I felt disconnected at times,

With what was realistic and

What could only remain in my dreams.

Spending a lot of time in my own head,

I'd go through all the things left unsaid,

Thinking of all the things

I'd wished I had said instead.

My loneliest hours gave me the ability to

Lean on myself and push through

This unbearable feeling,

While we all feel alone sometimes,

We are less alone than we think,

So when these feelings come to head,

Breathe in deep and find your grounding.

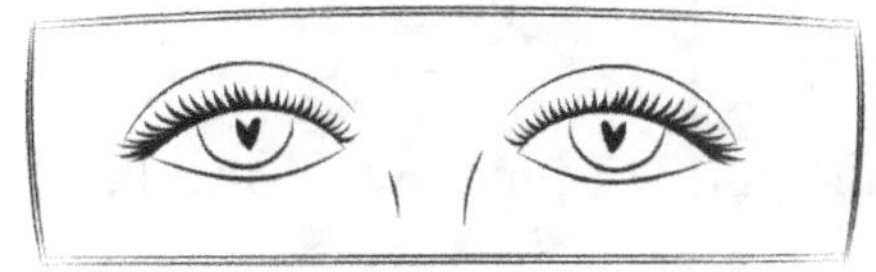

Heartache To Heartbreak

Broken and yet to be mended,

Through heartache to heartbreak,

Her smile breaks in half.

Her head aches as her body shakes,

Into the darkness, she's consumed whole.

Alone in the silent forest,

She weeps and hears no one,

She grows cold and distant

As her cries echo louder than she can bare,

Pain surges all throughout her body,

But as the night turns to light,

You can see her in the garden,

Dreaming of better days.

Night's Promise

For a moment there,

I lost myself in silence.

Sleepy-eyed and tongue-tied,

I open my window to feel the

Night's cool breeze.

This night promises sweet dreams,

Dreams that turn into fairy tales.

As I drift into my slumber,

I feel content with my life.

A smile curls up onto my face and

I know that I am exactly

Where I need to be.

Lovesick Fool

I get lost in his eyes

Like a lovesick fool,

I swim through his ocean blue eyes

And feel the deep depths of his soul.

I feel embraced every time he comes near,

And with every chance he gets,

He tilts my head and steals

Kisses from my lips.

He gives me that feeling,

That "head-over-heels" feeling where

I can't help but grin from ear to ear.

It's like jumping off a cliff,

Exhilarating and terrifying,

But I know I will not hit the ground.

I know that I am always safe in his arms.

Sorbet Sunsets

Swimming in the sorbet sunset,

I rest my eyes upon my love,

Tenderly, he kisses me.

I lay myself next to him and

Breathe in deeply,

The blossoms around me

are blooming in full,

Just as my heart beats for him,

I hear hummingbirds beat their wings,

I am soaring,

I am floating,

I am guided by his aura,

I find calm in his embrace,

I trust his strong hands to hold me,

His blue eyes to sedate me.

I am floating again,

Nothing beneath me,

Just air beneath my wings.